Whose Place

DATE DUE

Demco, Inc. 38-293

MAY 1 8 2010

Lydia Cortés

Whose Place

2009

Straw Gate
Philadelphia

Acknowledgements
Special thanks to Lilla Lyon. Thanks also
to Arthur J. Newman and José Pacheco.
And, of course, mil gracias a Phyllis Wat
for her ongoing support, encouragement,
friendship. Some of these poems were first
published on the Internet in *Press 1* and
through blogs of The Poetry Project.

Cover Art: Félix Rafael Cordero
Cover Design: Noam Scheindlin
Author Photo: Sonia Sehil Scheindlin

Straw Gate Books
44 West Washington Lane
Philadelphia, PA 19144

To Mami y Papi
Esther Mercado y Federico Cortés
who started it all...
and Lewis Warsh

Contents

Loss in the Family

Once I loaned 30 dollars to a young Mexican
who came to me via Italy, a girlfriend of a friend—Pio—
of my then future ex-husband

On her way from Roma to Monterrey via
New York she didn't have a place to stay so called me up from JFK—
Pio had given her my number not that I'd known it ahead of time—
still, I said okay, come on over

Though I told her the bus was much cheaper
from the airport she came all the way by cab to my East Flatbush place
She was very simpática…kind of attractive in a non-stereotypical
Mexican way…blond hair, blue-eyed but had a slightly crooked mouth

By coincidence she had the same last name as me
spelled with a final s instead of a z, the way it's *supposed* to be
though unlike me she came from money, planned to be a lawyer

Anyway Aida—that was her first name—
(like in *ay, ay, ay, ay, canta y no llores*)
not A-**EE**-Da (pronounced the American way)
stayed at my place more than the 2 days she'd originally
said she'd need, we'd agreed to, but was such a good listener
advice-giver, so sympathetic about my impending breakup…
she ended up still being with me a week later
I was about to throw a big party
in what would soon be my own apartment—

11

just for my little boy and me—
to celebrate my separation from my Roman husband of 5 or 6 years
I'd invited so many people I hardly knew
but I wanted everyone to know that I was definitely free…
or at least soon to be available

Two or three days before la gran fiesta I subwayed it
to the city from Church Avenue to Balducci's in the village—
a big deal for me—bought an assortment of fancy cheeses
about 15 pounds, spent a lot of money, just for the special occasion…
I'd never heard of some…Port Salut, Stilton stick in my head…

Some made quite a stink and I couldn't wait for the party
to begin but about 12 hours before the start of the bash
my father died of the cancer in his lungs
he'd been lingering with for weeks and naturally everything was
   cancelled

though for a while I thought I'd go on with it if it weren't
for the negative reactions that would come my way from the family
I knew they wouldn't come to the affair…

Did I give my sister the smelly French cheese?
I couldn't eat something with that degree of decay…though I did
manage the wine cheddar
Aida was at the wake with the family
met all the cousins from New York and Puerto Rico—
she spoke Spanish and private school English almost equally well—
everyone loved her stories, the clown faces, how she could screw up

her mouth more than was normal and in those hours of mourning
she almost became another member of the Cortés family

Of course, she was already a Cortés—
which incidentally means polite in Spanish, or courts, the judicial kind—
that is if you should remove the accent over the e

She left a day or two after the burial
and I never got a card nor letter, never saw nor heard from
Aida again nor ever got back my thirty bucks for her cab fare to leave

La Bendición

Never forget to ask
Mami and Papi
for The Blessing
upon leaving home, when returning
Expression of a beneficial wish toward
a loved one, especially to a daughter or son
Protection guaranteed in repetitive utterings
in virtue of the magic power of language
La bendición, Mami?
Que Dios te bendiga, hija
Que Dios te bendiga, nene
Gracias, Mami,
que Dios te bendiga.

Voces en Familia

They started out in Williamsburg. It was in the forties.
The kind father, Papi, worked in a cafeteria.
There was a mother, the Mami, two little sisters.
The Mami was depressed, the bigger little sister, a dreamer.
The smaller little sister, brilliant.
The long awaited boy baby, Freddy, a cherub, rosy, yellow
    eyes vacant, rocked, babbled, and rocked and rocked

after the evil dog at two the little brother stopped talking not the
right way never spoke ever after making sense making sentences or
phrases never not in english or español wasn't his fault fault whose

his voice shut off scared by evil devil's dog made the boy's voice
disappear he became the *seek* boy and his older sisters still little
girls couldn't believe in miracles the miracle milagros of the voice
returning to the little brother getting healed getting well no longer
a *seek* boy

the bigger little sister and the smaller little sister were supposed
to/should've believed in the church all saints on marcy
avenue gone to more masses gone to any pentecostal church
miracle storefront miracle store-bought any meant/means to heal
that might cure the boy the cure la cura the cure Ave María
Purísima ay Dios mío believe believe believe said the papi believing

in chants/incantations his formulas from el libro de san cipriano
his treasury of sorceries st. cipriano the papi said the saint says
nothing that exists is useless

that everything is so intimately united that if any one of the
elements were to be missing the universe would get so unbalanced
it would make us all stop existing

except the papi didn't say it so fancy he didn't use words like
intimately or unbalanced or even any of those in english the revival
healer men in the tents used yelling *heal heal* and some sick ones did
start walking without the crutches some blind started seeing some
with no voices began talking but not Freddy never in any tent so
other healer men who didn't speak english came to the house
whirled around white robes flying smoked cigars mumbling jumbo
mumbo jumbo hardly Spanish

that night of cigar fog and white robes twirling around the little
brother both the bigger and smaller little sisters hid behind el sofá
behind eyes glazed with disbelief fear believing it their fault theirs
la culpa suya culpa the brother didn't get healed well culpa grande
when the mami and the papi told them cure la cura la cura needed
the power faith la fe de la fe de la fe de toda la familia not just the
mami and the papi but the girls couldn't believe so the papi said
quizás maybe could it be the big and small little sisters wanted him
the baby brother sick siempre enfermito y…always inocente Freddy

api New Jeer bring in the New Jeer full of ron el barrilito barrel of
little fun rum making the papi happier redder than un Taino un
indio coloraó api New Jeer the papi forgetting the hours on his feet
cutting vegetables washing dishes in the jewish deli on delancey

hours horas y horas later still standing in his own little store la bodega he named La Fortuna

naming it to make it lucky make his fortune his veins varicosed bursting in air oh say can you see the New Jeer happy papi Feliz Año Nuevo como el huevo which came first el pollo or the eggs

in the bodega no chickens except for dead ones cold at rest in the big nevera near where the papi had the wood block must've weighed two hundred pounds there the papi chopped pork chops and lo' bifteks and ground beef on the side of the block a grinder a metal funnel with a handle he turned with one hand while the other red one pushed raw hunks of meat deep into the grinder's mouth with the smaller little sister always scared one of his fingers might disappear come out mixed chopped meat block was behind the great big fridge bigger than las hermanitas they were smaller than la nevera

behind them looking like un angelito the little brother one day found the kittens nesting in the box the papi had made for the mama cat who took care of the rats in the bodega for her and her babies but before you could know it the little brother Freddy took one baby out the nest flung it up smack against the wall with all his mighty might plop for a second it stuck to the wall the blood and guts pasted on that wall por un segundo before the thing slid down with a messier plop on the ground lay still between the icy nevera and the bloody butcher block where papi chopped and ground meats up

no es culpa suya la culpa the papi said he's a *seek* boy he doesn't know better el nene no sabe no doesn't know what he does not his fault God doesn't see his faults the mami said Papa Dios didn't give him anyway can't do wrong because instead he gave Freddy the sickness la enfermedad God with the sickness marks makes el niño inocente so he'll go to heaven be with Him Papa Dios forever and ever ah-men may God bless may la Virgen

María Purísima favoresca al nenito Freddy y papi ya papi ya papi y Api Happy New Jeer Freddy the little boy was 8 when the cats

Freddy's voice at 2 went away said the mami said the papi said before that said el nene was fine spoke normal till 2 they said it was the dog made the voice disappear like magic como la magia negra so the boy never talked never talked again not really only made some sounds like mami mami ya and papi papi ya ya after every-thing ya water was api api ya ya meaning already like ok already enough already i've said my word ya said it already papi ya mami ya api ya titi ya soda ya candy ya cay key ya pan ya pan the pan was Wonder

once the bigger little sister dipped a slice of Wonder in Pepsi and instead of calling it macaroni called it make believe Valencia cake cay key so Freddy learned to say cay key ya since he also liked cakes from Valencia in the bronx there was a cousin from puerto rico new to new jork Güicho lived in a basement on fox st. with his family cousin Güicho wanted bad to be american yankee doodle dandy didn't matter his mami cooked only comida puertorriqueña Güicho put whatever between slices of american Wonder made pork chop sandwiches plantain tostones y maduro sandwiches y de arroz y habichuelas the rice and the beans spilled out of his sanguishes and he couldn't help the accent

the mami on Sundays made carne mechada got a nice piece of beef
pot roast took a long sharp knife stabbed the meat attacked kept
turning it stabbing stabbing making slits the width of the knife an
inch all over cubed up a slice of ham thick the bone in edged white

fat all around cubed it up stuffed those ham chunks into the slits
pushing them deep into the meat pushed stuffed olives with red
pimento centers pushed little green capers in in as far as they'd go
put meat hunk in a deep pot browned it all around it sizzled in
olive oil and chopped onions chopped garlic added bay leaf can of
tomato sauce un poquito de sal added water turned up heat till it
bubbled turned down heat covered it up with pot's

heavy cover let it bubble bubble started smelling good invaded
nostrils made mouths water took off the cover she stirred it covered
it again the mami went to the bathroom that was when Freddy the
little boy the seek one came lickety-split opened the pot in a second
threw in the Ajax shook shook till whole container emptied
sprinkled white powder gurgled into red tomato bubbles more
bubbles more bubbles red pink sauce the smell a mixture of bleach
tomato bay leaf orégano powdery white over the red pink bubbles
quite pretty and strange

from the mami the bigger little sister and the smaller little sister
learned to recite a poem at 5 and at 4 and how to stand dressed in
lace on a box the papi made for their daughters from leftover
la fortuna crates to recite the mami's poem by heart and how to
put their hands on their hearts when the word love came up or
move them round in fluttery circles when love didn't come up from
the mami who made them pretty in lace and bows in their long hair

and together both little sisters recited for family for friends on new years and christmas or birthdays at all apartment parties the poem telling how good little girls las hijitas buenas should love their mami by heart…

La rosita cayó en el agua
The little rose fell in the water
La rosita perdio sus petales
The little rose lost all its petals

Mi mamita me quiere mucho
My sweet mother loves me so much
Pero yo la quiero más
But I love her more

Divine Bride

The girl in the photograph is no bride.
In black and white the girl smiles,
wears a white dress. A fantasy full of lace, Hail Mary.
She has a veil with a crown on her head
made of paper flowers, not thorns like the one
worn by the calendar Lord hung in the family's kitchen
Our Lord, her betrothed, as some might say.
The girl's palms exposed in see-through gloves
rest on the table. In their seductive hollow
lies a tiny rosary-draped book.
The girl studied that Catechism hard. At twelve—past her prime—
she barely learned the lines for her part. Then soon after forgot.

The day of the picture, the girl took First Communion.
The girl is not smiling happy she's about to be a bride of Christ...
if that's what *taking* First Communion means...
but aren't nuns Jesus' true spouses? Spice?

The twelve year old smiles all made up in rouge, dark lipstick.
She got to wear white stockings, little heels.
Looking like a bride was enough.

Not much changed on her wedding day.
In the portrait, she was posed in profile, solo in the shadows.
The girl smiled making a divine bride. Learned her part. Forgot.

Quinceañera

fifteen   sugar   cubes

        knotted

      onto silky   pink ribbons   the corsage

           pinned   on my   light dress

                hung

                                       d
                                       o
•   w
•   n

                                heavy

                      •

                          family grief

        in   sunlit   kitchen

                though   no   one

                        had

                        died

                        still
      Mami   stared away   stared

           out at

                blank

b
r
i
c
k

I tried   celebrating
    the   birthday

                                                  alone

when we're

gone   *you*   *will*
                    keep

your   *sick brother*

their apparent   mystery finally

        resolved

          she and Papi
               revealed

      that   I   should

         love and keep   my   sick brother

                   ....
               he   :::: *shimmers* ::::
                   ....

          they
          insisted
          shining
       their
          mistake on
      me

23

Marble Floors

In Italy
                    almost   alone
                                                    almost
                                at home
        a studio apartment

        a side pocket   bedroom

alone almost with   a kid too little to talk to
                                        with me
                I was empty   in Italy

over and over   I washed the same floors   cold marble
                I had   nothing
                                                better

                                                to   do.

Mi Adorado

The taste sweet
in my nose
the smell of his eyes
the sound green
the touch seen
plump my baby's feet plump
los labios de mi adorado
their suede persuasions
slide seep into the pores
of my caress
oranges and bacon frying

I Hated Lydia as a Kid

Lydia's not a cute name.
Looked it up—Lydia means *ancient country in*
the northwest part of present day Turkey on the Aegean Sea.
Who could be popular with a name like Lydia?
At home, they called me Lidín…what the hell was a Lidín?

Then suddenly, one day my lovable sister Sonia became Sunny
as if her disposition wasn't already enough appeal for the boys.
I was considered aloof. I was easily frightened. So shy.
I couldn't even shorten Lydia to sound friendlier, better.
More down to earth. What kind of nickname would Lid be?
That's worse than Lydia.

In other languages, like Spanish or Russian,
Lydia sounds glamorous, pronounced Lee-dee-ah.
But in American English the d is pronounced like the t in butter.
How unrefined. Some say Lydia is sophisticated. Guess they never
    heard Groucho
Marx sing *Lydia, oh, Lydia, oh, Lydia, oh, Lydia, oh Lydia the tattooed lady.*
If you want classy, isn't something like Dalia more elegant, lighter
    than Lydia?

I liked American names like Susie, Susan, Sue, Patty, Peggy,
Peggy Sue, Jane, Mary, Mary Jane, Annie, or Connie…
Not even in my dreams could I ever be blond or blue-eyed—
not as a Lydia—though even my cousin Milagros
pulled at least one miracle turning herself into a Millie.

White Queen, White Princess

Inspired by Cuban national poet
Nicolás Guillén's "Mulata"

So I have no idea, White Princess
White Princess, I don't know
If you can deny that
I have a nose thin
as a cigarette holder.

But don't look too closely
You are so far ahead of me
Because your mouth is so tiny
You don't pass for black, all washed out.

So little steamship your body
So little steamship
So little with your mouth
So little steamship
So little steamship with your eyes
So little steamship.

If you didn't know, White Queen,
The pretense
That I with my White Princess have,
That I love you with all I have.

Realist Painting

I look at myself
on the 4 x 6 foot canvas
over thirty years ago glorified.
Me, seen head to just above the knees,
looking a bit sullen, newly divorced, yet striking,
hair reaching below shoulders,
streaks just beginning to whiten my temples.

The painter, Richard, a cousin my age
and gorgeous, accentuated my cheekbones,
my lips, the bump on my nose, the veins
down my arms, on my hands hanging limp—
I look almost alive.

Richard is dead since 1989. He was one of the first.
Till the last months, who knew he had it?

In '74, he finally asked me to pose.
Thrilled, I'd wondered if he'd ever want me.
A year before he'd painted my sister—Sonia—
in black, dramatic, commanding, cigarette
dangling in her left hand, with Jane Fonda
anti-war short hair, big eyeglasses.
His portraits hung in galleries, even the subjects
got reviewed—why not me? Why not me?
When it came my turn, he told me to wear a diaphanous
two piece thing bright with green and yellow flowers, the

outfit I'd worn, belly partially exposed,
at the birthday party I threw myself for my thirty-second.

He posed my body three-quarters facing front,
but head almost in profile—only a bit of my left eye
is visible over the bump in my nose.
He made me come across stunning posed against
an old wall of the Park Row loft he'd sublet that summer.
He paid equal attention to that beat-up wall, its
indentations, the inconsistencies in color and shadings
as he did to the tiny flowers on my outfit or me.
Richard, the super-realist.

My girlfriends all had the hots for him.
He had exquisite manners, a real gentleman.
A handsome, dark, tall New York Puerto Rican
who spoke perfect English, who they assumed available.
But he chose me to be his model and I was
happy to pose for long stretches since
I wanted to please him, make sure
I'd end up astonishing.

During our sessions he was single-minded.
Out of the corner of my eye I saw his intensity.
What a great face, what a great model he could've
been. Too bad I couldn't paint…paint the way he painted me.

We had only two weeks to finish.
I was going to Europe, and by the time
I returned his sublet would be over.
So early each morning, from Spring Street

there was the long walk further downtown
to the old loft on that narrow street where
Richard prepared little meals for us—almost gourmet—
lovely breakfasts, sometimes with croissants and
later a delectable lunch, maybe an omelet with ripe tomatoes.
I enjoyed talking with him about art or fashion
about his siblings and parents or mine.

Still he never revealed much, not in reality, and I didn't probe
though in my bones I had always known more than he thought.

It got hot around ten and for the rest of the day the noisy
industrial-size fan on a stand was our only relief.
I held a pose for 15 to 20 minutes at a time, muscles stiffening.
He always asked if I wanted a break, but back in the
summer of '74 I knew there wasn't much time and
endured the pain to become immortal.

Obsessed with Class

Hereby I stand a
not quite brown almost white
person who doesn't even "look"
Puerto Rican who comes from
the working class…it sounds as
if I'd suffered for it. Does it make
me more exotic?

Give me a break…did I ever, did my sister
work like our dark Papi big handed red wide footed
legs tired veins popping from hours and days on his feet
full of corns Ave María washing dishes short ordered cooking
in a Jewish deli on Delancey, amen.

Before that in the fields of
Peñuelas in Puerto Rico did he
Cut cane or ñame or dig for yuca amen

Was I or my sister ever humiliated
for speaking an English nearly
unintelligible, laughable

Later he toiled in his own bodega
What good fortune to find it on Park Avenue
in Brooklyn near the family's fifth floor walk-up
to be able to buy the tiny store used
by lo' americano' only in emergencies

since we stayed open late but back then
only us hispano' used the word bodega
Now everyone, even white kids new to the city
say "bodega" like they invented it and that's weird

But back in the '50's and the '60's
there was Papi so proud of his bodega
with such reverence for it he gave the
place a name as if it was one of his nenes

He christened it La Fortuna
La For tu na   La Fortuna
Enough of a fortune so he could
send both his girls to study at St. John's
a private college because that's what they
wanted and las nenas usually got their way
but then again it also kept them *en Bruquelín*
close to la casa y la familia
Las niñas acted middle classed
acted good enough learned to become
almost americanas de veras…almost… taught
ourselves to get rid of the betrayal of the accent
though all was clearly seen when trusted friends came
to visit and met their Papi y Mami
maybe even saw—when he wasn't hidden in the back—
the weird rocking brother rocking snapping
his fingers clickety click how he made
strange sounds like some unknown
animal wounded
Saw the shiny paint each room

a different color the cracking plastic
covering up the sectional…el sofá moderno so
americano the family was so proud of las nenas
had pleaded por favor to have it for the Papi to buy
it till the Mami and the Papi threw up their hands and did

Ay Dios mío, ok, ok, que muchachas más mal criadas…
the Mami and the Papi ended up being right tenían razón
about the couch as the sofa sections slid apart one from the other
cada minuto you couldn't sit tranquilo you had to keep adjusting
getting up to fix or put it back together

Then just
a few
months
later the
sofa's
skinny legs
starting
shaking
fell off
one by
one
under
the
weight
of the
family

Wine Because Wine

Vino porque vino porque lo trajeron, Mami used to say.
Wine because wine because it was brought.
Porque vino mean came, ju know, but vino, also it mean wine!
Is funny, no? she asked.
She smiled at a joke older, sillier than she.
She smiled alone. I drank alone.

Vino vino. Wine wine. Came came. Vino divino.
Wine came and went. Wine went when it was brought.
Wind. Gone with. Why whine?
Sometimes I was wined and dined.

All wound up. A wind-up doll.
Wounds wind up opera. Wounds
covered up. Full of less.
Is funny, no?
No.

No, Mami never drank. I rarely smiled.
Melancholic alcoholics. Not funny.
Vino porque vino porque lo trajeron.
Puerto Rican wine is so syrupy, made out of pineapple.
But Mami said, *Our fruit is so luscious, so nutritious.* So said Mami.

Real (Mi Autosicografía...After Pessoa, Parra and Shailendra)

At home in Brooklyn we spoke Spanish
In school I was a learn English learn English learn English
Crash course pretend Americana
hoping people would believe
American I could be

The word *real* means royal in Spanish
Sometimes I pretend I am real can be
a royal pain I can fake my pleasure
Can fake being a real poet
in 3 languages royally

In Italy being *Porto Ricana*
was better than American unless I
could turn myself into a cowboy
Allora? Why not be an exotic
from Puerto Rico an island
most, even me, know little about?

Then I learned *Italiano* so well most natives
assumed I came from some place
just outside Rome
never quite sure

who I was
so good at my act
Once I prayed kneeling
beneath a tremendous crucifix
Christ winked smiling at me
I ignored Him
Even in dreams I make believe...

I don't see things
hard to fake faith or being a poet

Loss and Found

The street is where often I find things.
Something found means someone else has lost
or left it behind on purpose like a down-and-out mother
might with her unwanted newborn.

Sometimes I take things I shouldn't,
don't need more to complicate my life. In streets
I've picked up dirty slips of paper precious with words,
even in alien languages though sometimes I do know the lingo,
like the note taped by the super to the foyer door written in his
childlike letters:

> *ees now hot wather. Tudey an tummoro.*
> *Cuestions. Pleese cal lanlor to his telefon.*
> *Tanks, Marco*

When the faucet ran hot again, I looked both ways, ran down and
tore the note off the door. I crumpled it in my palm. A stolen gem.

Sometimes it's a small drawing. Who knows whose doodlings or
squiggles have slid into my pocket to be examined for significance
later. On the floor near my computer I find an old envelope with
some mysterious words. Don't remember when or why I wrote but
I like them enough that they'll go here:

if you can have peas and carrots, why not figs and carrots?

In the Great Hall of Cooper Union, I found three pens on the floor. It was during a talk on the gradual eroding of civil liberties in America. How lucky! One by one, I rolled the pens toward my foot, made sure no one had caught my greed, and stuffed them all in my bag.

Pennies are a dime a dozen. So many on New York streets that I rarely take them. Still I've not forgotten the mantra of the one man who lasted me nine years:

Never pass up a red cent or a black one (like me, he'd say)...maybe, baby, they'll come the day when all you need is that penny but since you don't stoop...what if you was high and dry but couldn't buy yourself a stupid water for that one dirty penny...Never pass up a red cent or a black one...

Sometimes I believe I've lost more than I've found, though that one man needed losing. But I've been lucky. I've found quarters in public telephone slots. I put in a quarter in a public phone one day and, presto, got back another three. Couldn't make the call though since the phone was out of order like my nine year man at the end.

Who and who and who found some of my favorite things?
I know I left the straw hat in the Oaxaca post office.

Where did the gold-threaded gypsy scarf roam
& what lucky so & so found my MoMa watch with its color-changing dial and who picked up my Balinese silver bracelet?

I spotted it from the subway platform on the floor near the seat where I'd sat but the RR's doors closed and it pulled away.
I couldn't do a damn thing.

And who ended up with the one time love of my life, the man I no longer wanted though we'd once sworn to be together forever. Seven years into it, my man's twelve-year-old came from Puerto Rico to visit. My man was proud he'd paid for the kid's ticket (never mind years of no child support). The boy said when he was three his mother threw his father out of the house.

Junior said, *"I heard Mami tell her girlfriend that was the last time she'd ever pick a useless thing out of the gutter."*

Ode to Simplicity, Attempted

Oh, Simplicity, I profess to want you but truly I love complexity
The extravagance, the excess of the genus lexis so my word choices
Tend toward the more exotic, even duplicitous, anything as long as
   it's about
Language, if one's not careful, the more tortuous, the more it can end up
As insidious as a city I'm so full of confounded insight. Shit?

That word's not found in some computers' thesauruses or are they
   thesaurii?
It's difficult to write an ode to simplicity when I'm obstinate
Adore all words, especially those which involve intricacy
Since I love tying myself around convoluted verbose conundrums
(Conumdrumni?) sometimes trying enigmatic vocabulary

Oh Simplicity oh straightforward times of Singers of patterns of Simplicity
Oh Singers I mean the old-fashioned sewing machines never fancy operatic
   ones
I confess I cannot write a simple ode to simplicity yet can address it
Pretty well as long as it needn't be in too plain a way

When I was a little kid finding my way through
The dense coppices of two languages Mami used to ask
If I wanted my milk   *con chocolate?*
                        o plein?
Sometimes I'd answer *Con plain.*
A little kid with two little vocabularies.

The Road to Bali

On the road to Bali in Indonesia, yes? we rode
On a two-humped camel—or is that a dromedary?
For many days through undulating passages lush with sand
Till finally we reached the jungles of Hope and Lamour the
Camel who we'd named Crosby did well by us but it'd been too long
Weeks on the road we rode we rowed that camel slowly eroding our
Provisions–oh, what we'd have done for a pan of water–not for Crosby–
He was still fine, dewy-eyed, dewy-tailed...but us? We were starving
And parched for agua y un poco de pan till my sweet Juan remembered
The satchel where he'd packed a...sponge...the sponge
The sponge that he'd smartly soaked with water, with water he'd soaked it
Hallelujah, we were saved and so rejoiced and had we tears we'd've cried
   crocs
In an instant Juan squeezed half of the sponge's contents straight into my
   throat
Then it was my turn to do him but he guzzled so fast he choked and died in
   an instant.

A House Like Two Dreams

Don't you know what I mean when I say talk down and dirt? The bark of the tree keeps the trunk. Still the text is deep, if not grave. Red is not tomb blue, green not pink crypt, black is not white; no thing is. Be real. Pray for me now. If not, then think of the cow. On your knees tell me you love. Do you call me great words?   Buy me fur. How, wh

en, where, but first what and why. This is not what she thinks. Does he hear? We come when they call us, not for him or her.   For you still. The cat, dog and bird make their home all in one place. I know not where. Do know why. Whose. A house like two dre ams. That was one. They are fine men, though they do not know how. Can I come with you,

like then, like once? We do it trice. This is no fun. Red ants do not mate with black ones. They just like what is like them. Is it gray or grey? Flavor or flavour? Flour o

r flor? Pour or por? Feel poor of words? Give me your pour, you're tiered, yours true blued. Which what is that which he eats? Are you a fool, a cloud? Can you rhyme like

you cry? No more will I ask a thing of us. I am scared. Scram. Like eggs, I do. You toast? Juice? Run? Eat right? No more, I said. Say what you must but don't ask, please. I beg. Did you today? Know why I love you just? I lie. I lie in my bed and think back to

old men in young days. Theirs. It might have been June, May,
March—

one of those. My heart. Draw me one. Pierce ears, just one. Please
cry. How could I? Love that old dog so. So what. Sew, sew your
pants. Your mom. Are you off? Will you be mine? Do not ask one
thing. Save face. Throat. Hand me your arm. Trunk and thighs.
Knees, legs and feet. Toes are safe too. Nails, if you have them.
Make a film. B

e one. The best bee. Can the ones you can't. See it my way. What
pays to be rich. Act poor. What a bad play. Play bad. Try to act
good. Don't have a fit. Did the glove fit the hand or the head? I
cannot go on. And on. Like time to give out. Play act. Act up. Do
a small part for man and the moon. See my keys? Don't talk back.
Not then. Come

eat. Come with me up to the sun. Come, eat. Do you care? Come
eat. Do you give one? Come eat. He will slap you. Come, eat.
Said that. KO MEH. Give up. Co me, eat. Tell more. Mami said.
KO MEH. There is not much time. Come, muchacha, eat. Right is
good, left is less than.

How to Stretch Panties

I lay upside down my shoulders between Geraldo's legs my head hanging over the edge of the bed and while he made love to me I commented that his bureau needed dusting.

I lay the right side up with Franco and looked him in the eye but asked whether he wanted red or black beans for dinner.

I sat on Tom facing him on a straight back chair and asked if he was inside.

I lay with my first cousin Russell in Manhattan. It should have been a simple sleepover after a late night party that would've made it hard to get back safely home on the subway to Brooklyn.

I lay across the bed with Ira over me and asked when he'd begin the driving lessons.

I stood up against a cold wall with John but he was too short.

I lay with Tony on a mattress on a bare floor and after great fore-play he fell straight to sleep.

I lay with Joe in a hotel and though he was thorough I thought about Theo only.

I lay with no one for seven years after a breakup.

I lay with Auguste in a red furnished room on his red lacy spread surrounded by wide-eyed dolls in crocheted red dresses. The bathroom was down the hall so when we were done he came back with a warm washcloth and said oh ma cherie! as he gently washed me.

I lay with George who squeezed me so hard it squelched my voice.

I couldn't lie straight with Tony. We were too tall for his car's front seat or the back and I wanted to stay a virgin so we just struggled and struggled and steamed up the windows.

I lay with a guy who broke wind near my face. He never said sorry so I wonder if he ever knew it or was just loose.

I lay with a nine-year-old girl who made me so hot and taught me so much when I was eleven. I pretended she was her sixteen-year-old cousin José who I had a big crush on.

I lay with Félix who surprised me with his proportions.

I lay with Manny in my head only.

DANGER
KEEP BACK
DEEP
EXCAVATION

I'm staying at a fancy hotel.

Do Not Enter.

It's upscale, with a spa. There's a guy by the pool talking to other workers. But he's not just a pool worker. Manager, I can see from the pin on the pocket of his white shirt though I can't make out his name. It's long with lots of letters repeated, both vowels and consonants. He sees me, gestures to me. Makes sure the spa attendants give me special treatment.

First Class Guests Only.

The staff fawns over me. The workers fawn, fawning beyond the call of duty, even at this posh place where fawning is a given. Their ministrations are more about making the boss happy. But, phony or not, I do enjoy the fuss, much as I hate admitting it. The manager is coming on to me but they pretend to not see. They are such good workers.

Employees Only.

I'm attracted to him. Hooked. He stares at me without shame. Doesn't seem to care the behavior is inappropriate. That only further arouses me even if I feel a twinge of guilt.

Keep Back.

I do so want him. I do make some half-hearted attempts to put him off.

Warning Men Working.

It's stronger than me. I'm aroused even now as I write, as I think of him. He's got that rare combination. Sexy and sexual.

Watch Out Falling Rocks.

He's at least 30 years younger than me.

Run Don't Walk. Run.

Thinking ahead, I'm a bit ashamed. What will he think? Of me, for letting everything happen…of me when he sees me naked.

Lights Out by 9!

Wish I had a body to show off, at least one with less flab and droop. Still, I'm not mortified enough to temper my feelings. I want him, and if he persists just for a second, which I count on, pray for, I'll collapse into his arms. I'm already ravenous for him, for his embrace, his mouth, his hands. My grateful body will respond to his in an instant. Ay Dios mío, me acting just like those zánganas in the pulp novelas, anxiously awaiting amorous attention, any I can get. I'm more excited each second. Ridículo. Yet desire, almost pain, is welcomed.

Danger High Voltage.

Yearning becomes almost holy. Ay, que románticas pero dolorosas those stories en las novelas! The man is slender but at least as tall as me. I call him *my man* though not to his face. He's dark. Is he East or *regular* Indian, Filipino, Burmese, Indonesian? He's more exotic than just Puerto Rican. So intriguing. We will end up making love. Where I don't know yet. He can't let go completely of the semblance of respectability in front of staff. My bones know it's not the first time he's muddled around with a guest. After all, besides being so charming, isn't he in the business of servicing? As I write, I'm aware how I slow down in the telling of the encounter. Wanting to create the excitement again? Is this why I take my bittersweet time? Oh, what yearning, oh, excruciating surge.

First Aid+Here.

I'm there. Now. The pool workers help me climb out of the warm pool, lead me into a white tent. Carefully, they roll down my wet bathing suit. Their eyes are impassive not allowing judgment into their gaze. They rinse my body off, splashing me with cool sweet water from silver buckets before gently wrapping a scented, heated towel around me. My man, mi hombre (that's how I think of him now in Spanish) enters the tent, coming to me. The workers move slightly away from me, making a space for him to get closer. His eyes are soft, self assured but not brash. Not overly. He adjusts the towel, the towel around me, tucks one of the ends tighter into the layer closest to my right breast. I shiver again when he brushes my hand first with his breath, then his lips. He steers me toward a door I hadn't seen before. He closes the door. There's a passageway behind it. I see it leads to a private elevator. He smiles wide and wraps his arm around my shoulder, rests his hand on my waist. I hold onto his left hand with my right. How warm we both are. We get off the elevator and pass many silent doors. At last, we reach my hotel room.

No Smoking.

I feel myself tingling and what I hear inside me is what I think a twinkling star must sound like up close, like the tinkling of a small bell. My cheeks are warm. They must be rosy pink as surely as is the moist place high between my thighs.

Caution Wet Floors.

He unlocks the door, leads me into my room.

No Trespassing?

He turns me toward him. We're face to face. We embrace arms tight around each other. The towel slips off my body. I glimpse my body in the bureau mirror, surprised it's not so bad after all. I'm not young, but my body doesn't seem to bother him. Or it does, but its good. He nuzzles my neck, covers my face, my neck with tiny kisses. Starts working his way down.

Warning: Persons with Pacemakers Stay Back 6 Ft.

He nibbles at my left nipple and then goes to the right. Works his lips back up. His mouth stops at mine. He kisses deep, his tongue probes hard.

Flammable and Explosive.

I'm so grateful. He likes kissing. He's very good at it. I cling to him, pull him down. We fall onto my bed, me under him.

Danger Deep Excavation.

My Nine Year Man

"Honeycakes, in bed I swear I'll always keep you snug up against the wall. Me, I'll be on the outside, arms nice and tight around you for protection. I know how to take care of mi adorada. You by the wall, me close to the fire escape…just in case a thief or some other delinquente ever had the nerve to try and get in… first he'll have this papito to deal with. Ain't gonna let no one hurt you. I'm the man. And if you get a hankering for something—I mean something you can't find in this bed—like a pill for pain from the bathroom or a chicken leg or hero from the kitchen—I'll get up and get it or make it. Anything for you, mi nena. Te quiero, te quiero tanto."

The stories got more convoluted, became lies, cheap novelas. Almost Tolstoyanas. If only she could still believe in fairy tales and happy endings. They both knew the score. They'd fought before. The last year was brutal, still they'd managed. She always thought there wasn't enough of a reason for splitting. Hard times and sticking together was what it was all about, he'd said. What was a little money (hers)…a little lying (his)? But finally she told him he needed to go. There followed weeks of teatro. Final scene? He left slamming the door. Out of her rent-stabilized almost Soho apartment, their nest for nine years. Left her standing, hands turning red in the steamy dish suds, hot tears dripping into the gaping sink. She looked up at the peeling, yellowed wallpaper facing her. How could he go? Who'd press his underwear now? Was there another mujer waiting in the wings? Otra mamita ready to flip his cakes, fry his bacon, tostón his plantains, bean his rice? French him up? She rinsed her favorite serving plate and lifted it out of the sink, noticing her fingers were starting to wrinkle in the water. The dish was slick with soap, with grease. She gripped it to her harder than she meant to. So hard it flew out of her weak grasp to come crashing down on the black cracked linoleum, where it crumbled. Too many pieces to ever glue back again. She pulled at her hair to hold on to something but letting go fell to her knees barely missing a raggedy shard. Splinters and slivers, fragments of shit. Ah, que vida melodramática! The word melodramática like melodrama for real. What a turn her life had taken. Left with useless pieces even after nine years. What a piece he turned out to be. Would she still dream of Frenching him up?

The Thing Loved

   La cosa   quería
The   thing   loved
               Otra cosa
            Another thing

    No la   cosa querida
   Not   the   thing   loved

Each   thing   went
          Seguía cada cosa

           Por su paso alegre

           Muy   triste
            era
 The   thing   loved
  The   love
      situation
   The   situation.

Guerrulona

War/raw/war?
Raw / war / raw!
ROAR
War.raw.war.raw.war on the worldwide web
Rawunderscorewar.com
Raw_war1@hotmail.com
War.raw@gmail.com
rawwar@aol.com
war&rawwar@yahoo.com
Guerrnika-a-ta-qa-
Guerra en guernica
Attak caca tak
Cacat.tack.atakata.@aol.com
Attakiraq@verizon.combat
Attak.afghan@usagangsters.org
Attak.vietnam@criminalsusofa.org
dropthebigA@japan.com
attak.haitianpeople@usacovertplan.com
attak.bigeuropeancities@wwIIusaplan.org
attak.cuba@enduringsanctions.org
bush-a-ta-
qa/\/\/\/\/\/\/\/\/\/\/\/\/\/\/\/\/=================
=========

mier-da- a-ta-
qa/\/\/\/\/\/\/\/\/\/\/\/\/\/\/\/\/=================
=========
fan-cu-l-lo- a-ta-

qa\/\/\/\/\/\/\/\/\/\/\/\/\/==================
==
a-ta-qa-a-ta-ka-shi-
ites\/\/\/\/\/\/\/\/\/\/\/\/\/\/==================
==
no-stop-pet-
\/\
/\/\/\/==================
a-ta-qa-a-ta-ka-sun-
nis\/\/\/\/\/\/\/\/\/\/\/\/\/\/==================
==
raw><war raw><war raw><war raw><war raw><war raw><war
raw><war raw><
$=><war? $=><war?? $=war><??? $=war><???? $=>< war?????
$=war><??????
*ratatata & ratatata $ ratatata & ratatata $ ratatata & ratatata $ ratatata
& $$$$$$$$$$$$ ra-ta-ta-ta
$$$$$$$$$$$$*

You Are Poised on my Belly Button

You are poised on my belly button.
You're amorphous, but well rounded
lips near all my main entrances expecting
my slumbered complicity.

I speak words of love of baby breath
oppression through pieces of broken mirror.
My words are frozen. You are magnificent.
Raw within chambers of sea water.

You're a hero, glistening trademark,
Dali's dripping cock trying to tell time off.
Kelp snake strangles nude in green desperation
exposing shocking pink departures.

Side by side, we are now both running
echoing alcoves of death.
Observers are positioned at a table
crude lives wanting out. Caring not about you
not caring about you nor about lovers
or the sea witches encircling your neck.

MTA Terrorism: Signs of the Times

If you see something, say something. If *you* see something, say something. If you *see* something, say something. If you see *something,* say something. If you see something, *say* some thing.
If you see, say.
If *you* say, see.
See you say.
You see something?

If.

If.

Say you thing some. See *something,* say *some thing.* Something *see,* something *say.* If you *say* see say *see see.* *If you* see say see *say* say. If you see *something, something* say. If you say something something say. If you see something *something see.*

Say, say.

   See, see.

    See say.

Say see.

See saw.

If you say, *see saw.* If you *see saw* say. If *you see saw* see saw. If you see see see say say say. If you see something, say something, see something if. You say if. You. You. You if say if something if see if.

If. If. Something. Something. Say. Say. See. See.
Si.

Si ves algo, di algo.
        Si *ves* algo, di algo.
Di *algo,* si ves *algo.*
Di algo, *si* ves algo.

Si algo si ves, si algo. Si ves, di.
Di algo, ves algo, ves di di ves ves si ves. Si di si di si ac dc eh see
algo ves algo? Si ves algo, algo ves.

If you see algo, di something.
Si you see something, say algo.
Si you ves
si you say, si, si, si!

You if.

See if.
If you see, if you see, if you see, if you see, if you say, if you say, say
something.

Some think. OK, think think, see? See, yes? Shout, enough. If you
don't see what there is not to see.
Si?
No veo, no veo, nada veo.
OK, can you see?
Nada.
Nada.

Black Was Pedro

Black was Pedro's color. He wore a black leather cap and motor-cycle jacket. Pedro never owned a motorcycle though. He said he was part of a special club of motorcyclists. Motorcyclists without motorcycles. It was a members only club but only he got to pick the members. Pedro's pants and beat-up shoes were black and his socks, when he wore them. The black started after Vietnam. He did it to mourn his time in Nam. He did it to mourn his mother. She died soon after his return.

Pedro's hair was black and curly. It reached his shoulders and a scraggly moustache and wispy beard covered most of the rest of his face. He wore a black wool cap pulled down to his eyebrows. Pedro was dark. A black Puerto Rican—really more a medium brown. Pedro wasn't at all tall or massive but with all that black, he did scare a lot of people. He slunk around quiet, his head buried into his shoulders which didn't help.

When he started writing poetry, some thought Pedro had gone loco in the coco.

Then Pedro started bearing a cross. He made the crucifix with two planks of wood nailed together. Held up straight, the crucifix was two feet taller than Pedro.

He painted his cross black, then worked on it more. He got hundreds of condoms—in all colors—and boxes of thumbtacks. He took the condoms out of their foil packages and nailed each condom ring to the cross with one thumbtack. Pedro tacked three rows of condoms up and down the vertical plank, three across the horizontal one. The tacks looked like bulls' eyes inside the rings. The rows stood out in rainbow contrast to the black crucifix.

He went all over town with his cross slung over his left shoulder. He took it on the subway, uptown to both El Barrio and black Harlem, downtown to Loisaida, even to Brooklyn and Queens. Pedro got himself mail-order ordained, became El Reverendo Pedro or Reverend Pedro. Soon a lot of people were calling him Reverend Pedro and not only friends and relatives.

He'd always had the power of seduction. Many women—and men—fell for him easily.

Pedro began carrying around a beat-up black briefcase. He made letters on both sides with white tape. One side said, *Reverend Pedro*, the other, *A Buck for a Safe Fuck*. Inside the case he put dozens of tiny manila envelopes—nickel bags—used for selling small amounts of pot. But on his envelopes he typed his own short poems. One said:

> *Woke up this morning, called my Equal Opportunity Employer.*
> *"Sir, I will not be coming to work today."*
> *"Why, are you ill?"*
> *"No, sir, I am feeling great. If I am sick tomorrow, I will report*
>   *early."*

Inside each poem envelope he placed a condom. He peddled the nickel bags—the poem condoms—out on the street, in subways. "Hey, people, check out my poems. Buy yourself a poem. If you don't like the poem, fuck it. At least, you'll get a safe fuck."

He used an old coffee can painted black to collect donations. He'd white-taped the can with the words, *Help Me, I Can See.*

Pedro scared people at first, but most ended up laughing. Maybe even thinking, without realizing they were thinking. But when people came across him alone in a dark place—or even in broad daylight—many turned and ran. He was weird-looking even for New York City. Still, Pedro had a laugh that caught you up in it, whether you wanted catching up or not. The laugh was loud, came deep from the belly and let out from a mouth opened wide to reveal the big gap between his front teeth and beyond. When he came across people he knew he'd explode into the trademark guffaws immediately calling out, "Hey, man, what's happening? Qué pasa?" And if they said, "Good," he'd shout back, "Far out" or "Out of sight."

One day Pedro almost got killed on the subway. It was on the F train. He was on his way to Coney Island, to a place called Side Shows by the Seashore. The ancient, falling apart theater was on the boardwalk and had been reopened by a young artist to feature a variety of acts. Mostly it was freaky-looking people who he'd gotten to agree to be looked at for small sums of money. A man whose face was completely tattooed (his closed lids had tattooed eyeballs) drove three-inch nails into his nose, cheeks and tongue. A three-foot tall woman dressed like a mermaid hopped around on her tail and said, "Hello, hello," while blowing bubbles. Another woman, normal in height but obese, roamed around, breasts covered only with a writhing python that she encouraged people to touch. A hairy man jumping around in a cage labeled Ape Man rounded out the "acts." And that day there would be Pedro. He was supposed to read and, he hoped, sell his Buck for a Safe Fuck poems. But when the F got to the Bergen St. station, three teenage boys got on the train. They wore baggy jeans falling off their asses revealing immaculate underpants, huge Nike t-shirts and caps with visors turned to the back or do rags. As soon as the boys saw Pedro, or rather, saw the crucifix with the rows of tacked up condoms and then him, they swaggered over to him shoulder-to-shoulder in close formation, hands already balled into fists.

"Yo, man, I'm Catolick, an' you makin' fun of my religion, cabrón."

"Yeah, man," said the one in the middle, "yo, you think Christ dyin' is funny? You don't never mess with Jesus. Fuck that shit, bro'." The boy made the sign of the cross, kissed his fingers, then balled his hand up again fast. "You lookin' to get *more* messed-up lookin' than you already are, huh, punk?"

"Word," said the third kid. "Man, you sure is some weird lookin' maricón."

Pedro's face drained, lost its rich brown. He talked fast.

"Hey, man, me, I wouldn't never mess with Jesu' Cristo. He's my main hombre too. He's far out. Out of sight. I'm jus' trying to tell it like it is…that, yeah, yeah, man, he *did* suffer for us… suffered so goddamn much… man, he died with those nails pounded deep inside him till he cashed in… we can't none of us take this life so easy… not any more man… we gotta take care of ourselves, us boricuas especially, ain't that the truth?

Two of the boys heard *boricuas* and relaxed a bit, let their arms drop at the sides… started listening. Then the third said, "I ain't no boricua, bro', I'm from the D.R."

Pedro kept talking… "Same thing, being boricuas, dominicanos, even some of them cubanos is like us… you know with la cosa de Aids, *La Sida?* We losin' too many brothers, too many sisters. You jus' gotta always remember to wear your rubbers if you wanna go play out in the rain, no?"

He opened the briefcase. Dozens of condoms fell on the subway floor...

"Free condoms, folks, free condoms for a safe fuck. A safe fuck for all. Have a safe fuck and have a nice day."

He let out the laugh, his laugh, and a few seconds later the boys, like others in the car, stopped looking scared, started laughing and scrambled to pick up the free condoms.

Ode to the Constant Spanish O...and the AEI y U

CheeriO O's r<u>ou</u>nd and hard but the American O
Is hardly steadfast like the O in Ode

<u>O</u>r as in eau de t<u>o</u>ilette watering itself <u>off</u> a French dirty t<u>o</u>ngue
Like the Oh! <u>O</u>ft uttered after a first kiss penetrati<u>o</u>n

Ok's Ok like the O in hellO but give the American Old heave hO Oh
T<u>o</u> - nO, n<u>o</u>t tOe - but t<u>o</u> b<u>oo</u>t c<u>oo</u>t f<u>oo</u>t s<u>oo</u>the s<u>o</u>d sh<u>oe</u>

Oh, American O!
Can't y<u>ou</u> make up y<u>ou</u>r mind h<u>ow</u> <u>ow</u> c<u>ow</u> br<u>ow</u>n

D<u>o</u> u Spanish u d<u>o</u> y<u>ou</u> want it y<u>ou</u>r American O?
FOe fee fi fumble y<u>ou</u>r slippery O's

SO h<u>ow</u> ab<u>ou</u>t hielO in which the h is silent
And the O less shOwy than any American O

YellOw w<u>ou</u>ld never d<u>o</u> f<u>or</u> hielO or Jell-O
Which is h<u>ow</u> <u>ow</u> Spanish speakers may prOn<u>ou</u>nce <u>ow</u> yellOw

Oh Spanish y<u>ou</u>r sweet O is l<u>oo</u>ser g<u>o</u>ssamer
Truer c<u>o</u>mes fr<u>o</u>m deep in a mellifl<u>uo</u>us thrOat

The españOl O is l<u>o</u>yal whether in Ode

O rOsa

O cOsa

O bOta

O bOdega

O gatO

O zapatO

O cOrazÓn

O teléfOnO

O amOr

O cOmputadOra jOdOna

O melodramáticO melOdicO

O OradOr

O embusterO

O maricÓn

O americanO

O es y será siempre O perO
Olé is not the same thing as Olay.

Reddish

In Public School 55
learning more and more
English
I was especially entranced
by words like the curious
reddish
and other words used during
those
Commie
hunting down
times
learned heard read words
red & pinko
& red pinko Commie
a lot
somehow I knew they were scary words
scary like taking cover hands over your
head and hiding under your desk in case
the
BOMB
came

One day the new word was
reddish
though reddish seemed friendly mostly
used to describe hair or clothing or
fall's turning leaves

I loved the ish of red or was it
redd?

Ish

is so Americanish

gibberish

Amarillo

I.	II.
Yellow	Spanish
is a	is a
color	language
What	Qué
is	cosa
color	es
Comes	este
from	idioma
where	De
this	donde
color	viene
thing	

III.	IV.	V.

III.

Things
are
things / cosas
But
qué cosa
son
cosas
Y por qué

IV.

Cause
leads
to
effect
Erase
the
cause
and
leave
what
thing
Effect
is
it
a
thing

V.

From here
to
there
takes
one
word
- to -
Qué
cosa
es
un
<u>to</u>
?

The thing of the thing is
La cosa, la causa
Because

To Pedro Pietri, Traffic Misinterpreter, Mr. Interpreter, Ms. Interpreter, Misinterpietri...The Reverendo

After Pedro's poem, Traffic Misdirector, *written in tribute to Jorge Brandon, Puerto Rican street poeta y declamador who carried his belongings around on the Lower East Side in a shopping cart and was rarely found without his caneca of Don Q.*

The greatest second living poet
in new york city
came to be and not be born
in Ponce Port of Rich but evermore of poor
his name is Pedro Pietri Speedo preacher
he is his own exaggerated and most underrated of metaphors
bearing crosses nailed crisscrossed with condoms
bearing also a black suitcase huge white lettered Reverend Pedro
glued to its sides
filled with poems typed on tiny manila envelopes usually used for
mari y juana except on his he typed his poems on the outside on the
inside one always found one condom...he'd hock them on the
street en el subway y en su high rise church
The Mother of The Tomatoes en la plaza de manhattan en la 43
saying "Man, if you don't like the poem think of it like this: you're
spending a buck for a safe fuck"...
what's more he carried a begging can that once held bustelo but
he'd covered in black paper and white masking tape letters
proclaiming "Help Me, I Can See"
en manhattan and y en puerto rico, nicaragua, o europa he was
way above way out of sight far out aloft he hovers still I feel him
declamando siempre estará and whoever cares to listen or not listen
he'll always speak con claridad this native boy de la playa de Ponce

from whence came Toña la Negra, la Bomba y la Plena they heard
him on spanish harlem street corners, in the east 105th family
church where he joined the Young Lords to protest injustice y por si
acaso invented his own iglesia la de La Madre de los Tomates la
poesía suya functioning one poesy telling truth for all the poor and
some rich below 96th street, stages on broadway's great white ways
and studios of hollowed wood holly wood were too depraved and
so were duly deprived of his sabiduría, only a little he did come to
be known (fuera de su gente) through some like José Ferrer, José
Papp, Raúl Juliá and even Paul the Simón, so Pedrito came to be
almost well known our Reverendo Poet
immortalized you now have to hang out in other spheres
though one'll still find Pedro Juan, the only one, El Único,
like Jorge Brandon, Pedro's own chosen
greatest living poet on rufos, escaped fires, en las barras, building
stoops en parques bodegas botánicas iglesias y quizás algún
sinogoga pawn shops card games cock fights funerals Valencia
Bakeries hunts point palaces and pool halls on orchard beach and
orchard street & cuchifrito stands on the lower east side which now
became upper the admission for his shows was casi siempre free su
presencia finally made the News and even The Times, with his obit
albeit in the saturday edition:

      su grandisima presencia el Reverendo Pedro
      his presence is poetry
      por siempre y amen.

A Patch of Land

I knew a man.
He wasn't a bad man.
The man lived in a small town in Puerto Rico.
The man, with his own hands, had built his own house.

The house was a little house.
The house stood on wood stilts on a patch of land.
The patch of land was on the side of a hill.
The hill was in Peñuelas. Some called it a *jibaro* town.
But it was fine, for the man was a proud jibaro man.

The man also loved USA.
The patch of land had been given to him.
Given to him by USA because he was poor.
Poor enough to get a patch of land.
The man loved USA.

He was proud to call himself a USA American.
He barely spoke English.
Understood more than he dare speak.
The man had once lived in New York.
The man had lived in Manhattan, the Bronx and in Brooklyn for years.
One time, the man almost lived in Queens.
The man never lived in Staten Island.
He had worked hard as a handyman.
Worked as a carpenter's assistant and painting houses.
The man had worked in many factories.

The man had worked at anything he could get.
The man stayed poor, despite all the jobs.

But the man always loved USA.
USA, he always said, had been so good to him.
The man loved USA so.
So much that nothing anyone said against USA could sway him.
The man, no matter what, was quick to defend USA.

He didn't want to hear about Vieques and the Navy bombing.
Didn't want to know about the pollution it caused on the little isle.
Didn't like to read about the cancers the maneuvers created.
Couldn't believe Puerto Rican women had been used in American
    experiments.
How could they have been sterilized without consent?
No matter the truths, nothing would ever make the man question the
    motives of USA.

The man loved USA.
Swore whatever USA did was for the good of the people.
The man believed USA was good as God.
So it was okay for Puerto Rican soldiers
to be sent to fight USA wars
in WWII, in Korea, in Vietnam,
in other unknown little wars and then in Iraq.
Sometimes a few must suffer for God and country.
He knew choice was never intended for all.
He said this was okay.

The man loved USA.
The man was asked what he thought about island Ricans—

including soldiers—not allowed to vote for president of USA.
And what did he think about all those Puerto Ricans
who returned from combat maimed or as cadavers?

The man thought a long while, took a deep drag on his Marlboro red.
He looked down at his calloused hands, the dark tobacco stained
    fingers, then smiled.

Puerto Ricans, the man said, *owe it to USA to fight.*
If they come back alive they're more than lucky.
And the ones who don't, do better than the live ones in some ways.
For in death, the man said, *they end up better providers for their families—*
more than before—if God wills it, maybe forever.

Didn't USA, the man asked, *give each dead soldier's family about 10,000*
    dollars?
That's what he'd heard...*That's a lot of money...how good is USA?*

The man loved USA.

Ripe Bananas

To Frank O'Hara

Am I a painter? I am not a poet.
Why not? I think I would rather be
a poet, am I? Well,

how about Alba Hernández
who's starting a poem. I stand to leave.
"Stand up and lack a swallow,'" she
says, "You can't have a long martini.
I can't play since I'm writing my poem."
I thirst; we thirst. I thirst slow. I'm
sightless. Try to avoid her poem.

"You put a tee shirt in it? But no TURTLES?"
She says, "I never thought of TURTLES.
It only needed a tee shirt."
"Oh." I come and nights keep coming
and I stand to leave again. The poem goes
no where, is never completed.
"No wear the tee shirt or TURTLES?"
Everything is there, so many pictures.
"It was nothing at all," Alba whispers.

And me? For years I don't think of
black: a ripe banana. I can't write a word
about a ripe banana. After years there
are no pages, even lines.

Now, no words. There should not be
so little of ripe bananas, so many pages

of silence, of how wonderful a ripe banana is
and death. The years stagnate. It's not even in
poetry. Am I a poet? My painting
isn't finished and yet I have mentioned
ripe bananas.

Stroke

At first he didn't recognize
the sound the phone ringing
an unfamiliar memory hesitantly
slipped between layers of air finally
it began to take shape in the end a ringing phone
was unmistakably what it was it was one hundred
percent a phone ring in one hundred percent real
air still sprawled out he reached over and picked
up the receiver...on the other end was...a man
a man so indistinct he might very well have
disappeared altogether to another place another
place a dim place that he could remember but did
not want to talk about for he...once was that man and
knew the place would never be a good one

Learned in my Mother's Kitchen

June 27, the last day of school when things are celebrated. Endings are celebrated for the oxygen and the liberty that accrues when the breathing returns and all seems content reminiscent of fulfillment inside a basket. Like the goodness of bread and the meanness of ice and the frills of dead lace or was it dead lice or cool ice?

Maybe I just need a vacation and it will work out because today feels like last day of school when learning commences and the night binges of magic will once more begin. And my strength will come back to fill out muscles of sagging limbs and sink or swim elbow skin hanging like sofas made out of someone's leftover leather.

Oh, what shall I say when someone asks why I try to talk all fancy as if that's the way I learned in my mother's kitchen. She stirred the beans constantly, staring only at the pot really hardly saw me there nearby the Formica table and I was so quiet as she said nothing to me. I wondered what she thought and that kept my mind busy and not so very afraid.

I was a good girl except that sometimes I lied. I made believe everything was ok because I didn't want to be noticed as the crazy one I knew I was. Mami was a little crazy sometimes and barely talked. My father and sister talked making sense always and seemed safe. Except when he was sleeping, my brother rocked on our velvet sofa pounding out dust and the springs. As if the sofa was a rocker he was on but he was off his. He rocked till he made a hole in the wall.

Plaster turned to powder, fell onto the floor, and behind the couch the slats of wood used to hold up the paint and the plaster were exposed.

The wall over the plaster was painted shiny turquoise. I hated the intensity of that turquoise but most of all, the shine and the shame. None of my American friends had ever put up with things like that in their homes. With parents who spoke an English as gaudy as our living room's turquoise. With a mother not crazy enough to know that her son was a little more than crazy. Later we learned we could hide him in the back rooms if we had to, when new friends came over. We were all in it together like one big happy family.

Still my brother never learned to talk. He only made weird sounds and holes in the wall. But when still little, maybe 8 or 9, he seemed almost normal abnormally beautiful, with big yellow eyes, hair golden curly, all cherub rosy. My mother, my sister, and I were on the greenish side of skin. My father was so red he could've been an Indian and maybe there was that in him, some Taino or Carib.

I couldn't take my brother for long especially when he got older and went through his changes, got bigger, stranger. We all go through changes when we get ugly before we get pretty again if we're lucky. But he fell out the window of our second floor kitchen and smashed his nose flat into his lovely face. The screams of my mother were hard to take too and I was afraid not knowing what to do—thank God for my sister—afraid to look out the window and see what my brother looked like after the fall. Mami had gone to throw out the garbage but just to make sure he wouldn't lose her, as usual, he leaned far out the window so he could see her as she fussed with the cans in the alley. But he went too far. Out he went of our yellow kitchen, he flew out to join Mami down in the alley. I never thought the shiny paint on our kitchen wall was so bad. Somehow it was happy yellow that they had chosen.

People know they're supposed to be happy. People can choose, so they say. People aren't happy even when they make believe if they know they're making believe. Is Milagros more than a name? To know, to believe, to hope, to be, to breathe, to run. To hide, to lie down and die. To stop.

The baby says, go car, go. The car goes. The baby goes go go. The baby grows inside the belly then outside if he makes it out. The baby grows if it's let live, helped a little.

With a little help from my friends I can make it with just a little I. I want to write with just an ear, an eye and a little help from my head, I.

Nails through the hands, feet make an interesting picture. All those paintings they made of him hanging onto that cross, nailed to it. The best fashion accessory was the crown. The thorns interwoven with such skill into that ring so lovely.

Holy water, Holy Jesus, Holy Ghost, madre mía, María madre ave mama mixed up cows and pigs and other hard animals. *They're animals. Can't they keep themselves clean?* Fed? Fed up and fit to be tied. Fed then tied up made to do things a pig would never dream of. Though a cow might, given the freedom of an imagination. Given freedom all things can be imagined even the taboo. A miracle? Boo who. How crazy is this kind of talk?

The son, the sum, the son, the sun always there shining over the little parallelogram house, one or two windows, a small door, one or two flowers in the foreground, a tree with three or four apples. And an s-shaped path leading to the door. My house never varied. Like happy endings. It was all very normal. That's how I was taught to make it. Taught eyes tight needing water to wash the dry away.

Whose place.

Lydia Cortés was raised Puerto Rican in Williamsburg, Brooklyn, and has also lived in Rome, with Manhattan her longtime home. She has been awarded various fellowships, grants and residencies. A number of Cortés' works are anthologized; poetry in *The Anthology of Puerto Rican Poetry: From Aboriginal to Contemporary Times* and in *Teaching with Fire.* Her story, "Home Cookin'," appears in the Beacon Press anthology *Through the Kitchen Window.* Another Beacon Press anthology, *In Praise of Teachers,* contains one of her essays, and Heinemann's *Monologues from the Road* has one of her plays. Cortés' previous poetry collection, *Lust for Lust,* was published by Ten Pell Books. Additional work is forthcoming in the *Anthology of Puerto Rican Women Writers.*